A
JOURNEY
OF FAITH

a dialogue Between
ELIE WIESEL
and
HIS EMINENCE
JOHN CARDINAL O'CONNOR

A
JOURNEY
OF FAITH

Based on and expanded

from the WNBC-TV Broadcast

FOREWORD BY GABE PRESSMAN

DONALD I. FINE, INC.
New York

Library of Congress Cataloging-in-Publication Data
Wiesel, Elie, 1928–
A journey of faith / by Elie Wiesel and John Cardinal O'Connor.
p. cm.
ISBN 1-55611-216-5 (alk. paper)—ISBN 1-55611-217-3
(pbk. : alk. paper)
1. Wiesel, Elie, 1928– —Religion. 2. Holocaust (Jewish
theology) 3. O'Connor, John Joseph, 1920– —Views on Jewish-
Christian relations. 4. Judaism—Relations—Christianity—1945–
5. Christianity and other religions—Judaism—1945– I. O'Connor,
John Joseph, 1920– . II. Title.
PQ2683.I32Z465 1990
261.2′6—dc20   89-46146   89-46320 (pbk.)
CIP
Manufactured in the United States of America

10 9 8 7 6 5 4 3 2 1

Designed by Irving Perkins Associates
Photography research courtesy of Barbara A. Borowitz, Image Visions.

FOREWORD

They come from very different backgrounds. They look at the world from vastly different perspectives. But Elie Wiesel and John Cardinal O'Connor share an abiding faith in God. And, when they speak of the Holocaust, they are deeply conscious of the uniqueness of this tragedy in human history and the need to remember it always.

It was Elie Wiesel's idea to do this program. And both the Cardinal and WNBC-TV readily agreed it was a good idea.

We sat them in front of a fireplace at a seminary in Yonkers and let them talk. The cameras recorded a four hour conversation. They needed only slight prompting from me. Essentially, this was a dialogue in which two men exchanged their ideas on issues of mutual concern ranging from the nature of evil to anti-Semitism, suffering, the existence of God and other matters.

For producer Clare Friedland editing the program was a labor of love and a mission of sorts—for she herself is the child of concentration camp survivors—and her mother comes from Elie Wiesel's home town of Sighet. "I kept thinking of my dead father and the one time in my life I had seen him cry—during a visit to the Holocaust memorial, Yad Vashem, in Jerusalem."

I think there is much for all of us in the Wiesel-O'Connor encounter. The conversation about God, life and love reaches a climax when the Cardinal reads to Wiesel from his own book. For the participants in the dialogue and for those who witnessed this unique event, it was a moment filled with tears.

—Gabe Pressman
Feb. 21, 1990

Gentlemen, we're approaching the end of a century of unprecedented violence and suffering. Each of you is the son, the descendant of a great religion. In a century of death and cruelty has it often been hard for you to keep your faith in God? Has it ever occurred to you to ask, "How could a just God tolerate this?" Mr. Wiesel?

MR. WIESEL:

Well, I had nurtured these questions for many years. I still have them. My questions are still open. But contrary to what some of my readers thought, I never lost faith. Even during the war, in those dark places, I kept on praying to God. And some of us even managed to put on phylacteries in the morning, in Auschwitz. My father and I got up an hour before everybody else. Somehow, someone had managed to smuggle in a pair of phylacteries, tefillin, into the camp. And my father and I would get up every morning and pray. Now, when I say my prayers, I cannot believe that is what we did then. The prayers are strange prayers. One of them, for instance, is *Ashrenu ma tov Helkenu*—How happy we are, how happy is our lot. Now, to say that *there* is inconceivable. And yet we said it.

1

MR. PRESSMAN:

Why?

MR. WIESEL:

Happy—happy, what kind of happiness was there? How could one speak of happiness, when the word itself had lost its meaning? No words had meaning then. And yet . . . So my problem, my crisis—there was a crisis in my faith—came much later. I think two or three years later. I began wondering: what was the meaning of all that?—which is the question of all questions. What did it all mean?

Once you ask this question, of course, God enters into the picture. Where was God? But I'm asking the question from within faith, not from outside faith. If I didn't believe, where would be the problem? But if you do believe, then you have painful questions. And these questions remain open to this day.

MR. PRESSMAN:

Your Eminence?

CARDINAL O'CONNOR:

Well, you're a questioner in all your books, Professor Wiesel. I would say every one of your books is a question in itself. It was interesting to me to read *Life* magazine some months ago, in which the question is asked of fifty people: what is the meaning of life? I wasn't surprised when I read your answer. You said, in part, "I ask questions rather than give answers."

The question of evil is a fundamental question for all religious faiths, for all philosophy. And there's nothing strange about it; you don't have to be talking about an "age of violence." There's always evil in the world.

In the third century, for example, the existence of evil was questioned by the Manichees, believers in a form of Zoroastrianism, the ancient Persian religion where everything was judged by two forces, light and darkness. These two forces vied against each other and there was always a question about which would win, the light or the darkness. The Manichees saw evil in many things. They saw evil in marriage, they saw evil in the relations between men and women.

St. Augustine was influenced by this form of thought. Augustine was a real profligate, a ne'er-do-well, born of a pagan father and Christian mother. Then he became a Manichee and he became totally absorbed in the problem of evil. It was not until he had abandoned Manichaeism, however, that he developed his own philosophy of evil. Augustine understood evil to be the absence of that good which should be present in all things. Evil, simply put, is the deprivation of good. For example, blindness, lying and murder are evil because there is a deprivation of sight, truth and life—the good which should be present according to the nature of things.

So even as far back as 434 when St. Augustine died, the question you pose was being asked. And we've been struggling with it ever since. It would be naïve to say we know the answer despite our attempts at philosophical explanations. The question for us is: if God is absolute goodness, pure truth—and this is what we believe—then how can there be evil? We attempt to explain by way of the concept of free will, the wonderful gift given to us by God. By the virtue of this gift, we choose between good and evil. But how did evil come into the world? We believe, from our theological perspective, by way of original sin, the primal act of pride on the part of the parents of the human race—

3

pride that drove them to try to usurp the divine will, pride which led them to believe they could become gods. How? Interestingly, by coming to be able to determine for themselves what is good, what is evil, apart from God's will.

It's very complex. But the problem often is that when you try to argue something of this sort, you argue it in these terms: "If there is evil, how can there be God?" I think I would ask instead: "How could there be God if there weren't evil?" God is just this fantastic mystery. Simply because we can't explain the existence of evil, doesn't mean that we necessarily then attack the question of the goodness of God. It's rather that we're extremely limited and we haven't succeeded in coming up with an answer.

But Professor Wiesel, you said something that struck me. You said that now in saying your prayers, at times you're stunned by the prayers that you could say in the horrors of the concentration camp. For example, you used the word happiness, "How happy we are." And Mr. Pressman asked, "Why?" I wasn't sure if he meant, "Why were you stunned at being able to pray," or "Why were you stunned at being able to say that particular prayer about happiness?" I would look at happiness as interior peace. And you could have interior peace under the most horrible circumstances.

MR. WIESEL:

Not there.

CARDINAL O'CONNOR:

Some people did. For example, Dr. Viktor Frankl, the Jewish psychiatrist who was imprisoned at Auschwitz, said in his book, *Man's Search for Meaning,*

4

"A thought transfixed me: for the first time in my life I saw the truth as it is set into song by so many poets, proclaimed as the final wisdom by so many thinkers. The truth—that love is the ultimate and the highest goal to which man can aspire. Then I grasped the meaning of the greatest secret that human poetry and human thought and belief have to impart: *The salvation of man is through love and in love.* I understood how a man who has nothing left in this world still may know bliss, be it only for a brief moment, in the contemplation of his beloved. In a position of utter desolation, when man cannot express himself in positive action, when his only achievement may consist in enduring his sufferings in the right way—an honorable way—in such a position man can, through loving contemplation of the image he carries of his beloved, achieve fulfillment. For the first time in my life I was able to understand the meaning of the words, 'The angels are lost in perpetual contemplation of an infinite glory'" (pp. 58–59).

Another example is Maximillian Kolbe, a Catholic priest who was condemned to die at a concentration camp. On August 14, 1941, an innocent man was condemned to death as compensation for an escaped prisoner. Father Kolbe resolutely offered himself to death to save the man he did not know. When Father Kolbe was canonized a saint by Pope John Paul II, the man he saved, Francis Gajowniczek, was present.

So I think that a person could find interior peace even at a concentration camp—as Dr. Frankl and Father Kolbe did.

MR. WIESEL:

Oh, I know some very religious Jewish survivors, but—
even they did not have inner peace.

MR. PRESSMAN:

So did you say it by rote? Was it just a prayer?

MR. WIESEL:

I grew up a very religious boy. The most important area in
my life was religion . . . When I came to Auschwitz in 1944,
I had in my bag more books than food. I brought my books
with me, thinking how can I live without these books? They
were all religious books. All were taken away from me—
but what kept me going was that I could pray by heart,
study by heart. And I had that passion for God as a child,
as an adolescent. I began studying mysticism at the age of
thirteen. And therefore there was no problem. That was
what I had to do. My identity remained almost intact only
because I was capable of saying the same words that I had
said before.

And after the war, I somehow closed the parentheses and
went back to do exactly the same thing—I recited exactly
the same prayers.

MR. PRESSMAN:

A character in one of your books says man raises himself
toward God by the questions he asks him. That's the true
dialogue. Man questions, God answers. But we don't understand his answers. We can't understand. What are some
of the questions you ask God that eluded answers?

MR. WIESEL:

Then? Or now? They may even be the same questions. I was always wondering. Again, the question that comes frequently to the lips of some of my characters is—Where is God in all that? I saw literally, I saw with my own eyes children being thrown into the flames. I don't say it often but I've written it in one sentence, once. Now, where is God in all that?

So I remember, I remember thinking: This is like the Inquisition. Or I remembered: This is like Abraham who was thrown into a burning furnace. I needed some kind of vantage point. I needed to be able to look back somewhere and find some kind of parallel. But the question is still there—Where is God in all that?

And even today there is so much hatred in the world. Hatred, unfortunately, that has some religious character, too. And I wonder: Where is God in all that? People who speak on behalf of religion and incite people to hate one another, or to murder one another, and I say, "Where is God in all that?"

CARDINAL O'CONNOR:

I think you know the answer, you have the answer. God isn't in all that. God isn't in any of that.

MR. WIESEL:

There we disagree, I think. Because first of all, in the Jewish tradition we don't believe in original sin. We believe we are all responsible for what we are doing *now*.

7

CARDINAL O'CONNOR:

But how can you say that God is in hatred? God is love. And I think that you asked the question brilliantly. You answer it implicitly, but then you don't accept the answer, because the answer has to come from faith. It can't come from reason. You must begin with "God is love" because if you begin by saying God is not love, then there's no point in asking, "How can God be in hatred?"

MR. WIESEL:

I didn't say that. I said where is God, God is everywhere. If God is everywhere, he's also in everyone. In every act. And in every thought, in every tear, in every joy. And in evil. It's up to us to redeem that evil. But if I say God is not everywhere, God is not God.

But again, the problem is, God is everywhere. There is nothing void of God. The mystical expression for it is *Leit ata panui minei.*

CARDINAL O'CONNOR:

But when you say God is everywhere in that sense, you must be careful to avoid being purely pantheistic. We say God permits the hatred, but God is not in the hatred, and certainly God cannot *be* hatred.

MR. PRESSMAN:

You made a specific reference, Mr. Wiesel, to the Ayatollah Khomeini calling for the execution of Salman Rushdie. And you said God was in that request for death.

8

MR. WIESEL:

Oh, I must tell you I am shocked; as a believer, I am shocked that a man who is the head of a religious movement could do that. I understand the sensitivity, I understand that so many Muslims were hurt by Rushdie's description of Mohammed. But from there to say, "I'm sending people to kill that man"?

CARDINAL O'CONNOR:

Of course that's not understandable or appropriate, but you can't say that's an act of God.

You could say it's "done in God's name," but that's a perversion. Many horrors have been perpetrated through the centuries in God's name that certainly had nothing of God in them.

MR. WIESEL:

In God's name, all right. But here—here, really, I'm not blaming God, surely not. I am blaming the Ayatollah Khomeini. But the fact is, he said what he said in the name of God.

CARDINAL O'CONNOR:

But you can blame God in the sense that you don't understand; you can blame God if you're giving a purely rational interpretation of God. But you can't give a rational interpretation of God. You can't put the ocean into that glass.

MR. WIESEL:

I can. I can. I think a person can drown in this glass. He doesn't have to drown in the sea. I can drown in one tear.

9

CARDINAL O'CONNOR:

You can put an action in the glass, but you can't put the ocean in the glass, again by definition. If God is infinite, as I believe, and there's no question but that we are finite and limited, by definition, you can't put the infinite into the finite or the limited.

They tell a story about St. Augustine. He was supposedly pacing along the seashore pondering the mystery of the Trinity—one God in three divine persons. Suddenly he came upon a little boy with a little bucket. The boy was going back and forth filling the bucket with seawater, then pouring it into a little hole he had dug in the sand. Augustine asked, "What are you trying to do?" The little boy said, "I'm trying to put the ocean in this little hole in the sand." Augustine said, "That's impossible." The little boy replied, "It's no more impossible than your effort to put the Trinity into your mind."

I don't begin to pretend to be able to encompass God.

MR. WIESEL:

I cannot, but God can.

MR. PRESSMAN:

Have there been moments, Your Eminence, when you wondered how God could tolerate the things that you've seen in your life?

CARDINAL O'CONNOR:

Oh, of course. One would have to be an automaton not to wonder. I would see no virtue in *not* questioning God. We are human beings with the divine gift of reason. This absolutely magnificent, brilliant gem of reason must be used. So when I look at what appears to be irrational, I have to question it. I ask the same questions that Professor Wiesel asks.

MR. PRESSMAN:

You mean even a cardinal of the Roman Catholic Church?

CARDINAL O'CONNOR:

Even a cardinal. I think a cardinal must be first and foremost a human being and use human reason. Let me explain this a little further.

We have two great gifts, the gift of reason and the gift of faith. My reason causes me to question and question. Faith doesn't give me reasonable answers to the questions, but it tells me that the question is beyond me, the explanation is beyond me, beyond my reason. But God knows. As St. Augustine said, "Credo ut intelligam," I believe in order that I may understand.

How does that work? I don't know how it works. Could I explain World War II, could I explain Vietnam, could I explain crack, could I explain the daily exploitation of people, the horrible persecutions? Could I explain the Holocaust? Could I explain any of these monstrous sufferings in the history of humankind? I can give a theological explanation that our human weakness is rooted in what we call original sin, inherited by the entire human race. That's an explanation; it's not a reason.

We can look at causes of things but not necessarily give reasons for their existence. I know that because of the sun and because of this wonderful process called photosynthesis, plants convert sunlight into energy by way of chloro-

11

phyll. That's an explanation of cause and effect. But why is there a sun? I can't explain the sun.

It's partially an act of reason. I can say that there has to be a being behind the sun, one that brought the sun into existence. But ultimately, if I'm going to penetrate to the nature of that being, this has to be an act of faith. And that's a gift.

MR. WIESEL:

I have one comment on that. We Jews don't blame God. We question God. I can blame human beings. And I do, and we should blame human beings when they do something wrong to other human beings. But to blame God, that's quite an act of arrogance. And we don't do that. But we question God.

CARDINAL O'CONNOR:

But we do blame God, I think. Of course we question in the profound sense of the term. But we are weak human beings, and we become irrational and we shake our fist at God and blame Him for that which seems so wrong.

I see so much suffering. I spend so much time in hospitals, so much time at funerals. I see women who lose their little babies; I see little babies who lose their mothers; I see husbands who lose their wives. And certainly many of them question God, asking, "Why?" But they also blame God.

I've heard people say, "God, stay out of my life. I want no part of You if this is the kind of thing that results." There's always that existential *why*. It's a questioning not only of God, it's a questioning of ourselves. Why are you? Why am I? Why do I do the stupid, inane things, the irra-

12

tional things that I do? How do I answer, except in terms of the mystery and the enormous potential of suffering?

MR. WIESEL:

It's strange, I know—when I look back in my tradition, we don't find that. Only once, literally only once, is there a reference to an attitude such as this. Bar Kochba, the famous hero, when he fought, actually said to an uncle of his, who was a great sage, "Please, tell God to stay out of my life. I don't want his blessings, nor do I want his punishment. Let him simply be neutral. I want to fight my fight alone."

That's why he lost the war.

CARDINAL O'CONNOR:

You find it in the Scriptures. You find it with Job's counselors, for example.

MR. WIESEL:

Oh, no. Oh, no. I'm sorry. Job's counselors, first of all, took God's side. They became [His] protectors.

CARDINAL O'CONNOR:

First they did, but it was a back-and-forth dialogue. The same with Jonas, running away from God. Jonas wanted no part of God. And look at what Moses did. Moses said to God, "Why have you given me all these people?"

MR. WIESEL:

Job didn't want God to be indifferent. Job was ready to accept God's punishment, even God's injustice, but not

13

God's indifference. Moses pleaded for his people at the moment God turned against the people. When the people were safe, or Moses thought they were safe, then he began chastising them.

God is always part of our experience. God must be present through everything we do.

MR. PRESSMAN:

The Holocaust, the horror of millions of people being put to death systematically by the followers of Hitler—what do you think it will mean to our children and our children's children? How will they look back at this in the next century and in the years after that?

CARDINAL O'CONNOR:

Well, I hope they *will* look back. If they don't, that could be the worst tragedy of all. In my judgment, it would be the greatest peril if the meaning of the Holocaust is lost, forgotten, dismissed or trivialized.

If they do look back, then so much depends on the way they're taught. They may look with that same indifference or disbelief that a tremendous number of people in the world exercised while the horror was happening.

MR. PRESSMAN:

How do you see it? You've been described as a prophet—

MR. WIESEL:

No, oh, no.

14

MR. PRESSMAN:

But you, you undoubtedly have looked ahead and wondered.

MR. WIESEL:

I am afraid. I am afraid of the trivialization of our tragedy. One thing is clear. This is the most documented tragedy in recorded history. We find no other tragedy or other event that has been documented from so many angles. The victims, the killers, the bystanders. Millions of documents. So the archives will be full. And if a hundred years from now people will want to know, they will know where to turn.

What will they think? I think they will think that society had abdicated. That culture was bankrupt. And it will be a commentary on history, that might lead to total despair. Whenever I study or explore that period, I find nothing but darkness and despair.

MR. PRESSMAN:

But you heard just this month, and you hear it frequently, a meeting, a so-called meeting on the West Coast, I believe, by a revisionist historian who claimed that the Holocaust didn't exist. He got an audience, I read, in the Los Angeles *Times*, of about two hundred people—but about that kind of revisionism, denying the very existence of the Holocaust.

MR. WIESEL:

Those are the most wicked of all people. There *is* anti-Semitism in the world, racism in the world. But the most

wicked of all are these so-called revisionists. They are morally ugly, morally perverted, morally sick.

CARDINAL O'CONNOR:

It's a cyclical kind of thing. Remember about fifteen years
ago, there was a move in the same direction. Some college
professor somewhere wrote what was allegedly a scholarly
book that said the whole thing was made up.

MR. WIESEL:

Unfortunately, the revisionists are all over the world.
While the ceremony of the Nobel Prize was being held—

MR. PRESSMAN:

When you received the Nobel Prize?

MR. WIESEL:

There was a demonstration outside in the streets. There
were people who said that it had never happened, that the
whole thing was a hoax, and so forth. Those people have
lots of money. I don't know from where. But they do. And
their books are being translated in to almost every lan-
guage in the world. You find them in Germany, in South
Africa, in Norway and even in Australia. Wherever I go, I
find them.

   Just as we are committed to preserve memory, they are
committed to distort it.

MR. PRESSMAN:

Is anti-Semitism as you perceive it, Your Eminence, a
major problem?

Oh, there's no question.

I think it's still deeply rooted in so many of us who are not Jews. It's even institutionalized in many respects. As with so many prejudices, we may not be conscious of it at given times or for extended periods of time. But it operates in so much of what we do and say at an unconscious level.

MR. PRESSMAN:

Institutionalized?

CARDINAL O'CONNOR:

I think it's institutionalized, yes. Thank God we now have from the Second Vatican Council a famous document, *Nostra Aetate* (In Our Age), which draws its name from the first three words of the document. It is an enormously important document on the relationship between the Church and the Jewish world, the Muslim world, non-Christians in general. Until the time of the writing of this document, some people gave very little thought to what was taught in our schools, in our textbooks and how we were rearing children.

As a church, we came to recognize through the impetus of *Nostra Aetate* and other efforts that some Catholics had literally blamed the Jews for the crucifixion of Christ, and this institutionalized within Catholicism itself a degree of anti-Semitism. I think, to our credit, after *Nostra Aetate* came out and our attitudes began to change, we began a long-range program to purge our textbooks of this kind of thing.

This wasn't revisionism; this was writing the truth for the first time. And the real perniciousness of anti-Semitism

17

was that so much was not intentional. So much wasn't deliberately, consciously articulated.

In another area of prejudice altogether, and certainly not limited to Catholics, is the fact that so many people literally believe that the Jews run the world, the Jews run the United States. There is still the mystique of a kind of "international cartel." Such thinking is totally unrelated to what Catholics may or may not have been taught to believe about the crucifixion of Christ.

There are some people who believe that every newspaper, every television station is owned by Jews. It's tragic, and it affects our thinking, and it affects us that much more perniciously if we deny that it does. I repeat strongly: such prejudice is by no means limited to any specific religious body.

MR. PRESSMAN:

This gives you great concern?

CARDINAL O'CONNOR:

It gives me very great concern. I preach about it a great deal. I seize every opportunity to get at it publicly. I can't count the number of times in my past five years in New York that I have lectured on or preached about anti-Semitism. And most of the time, I'm trying to get at unconscious anti-Semitism.

I meet with various Jewish groups and with rabbis. I meet with representatives of Jewish agencies. We're constantly trying to get at not simply anti-Semitism, but at the relationships between Judaism and Catholicism, or between Jews and Catholics and, it must be said, anti-Catholicism on the part of some Jews.

18

MR. PRESSMAN:

Do you have great concern about anti-Semitism right now in American society?

MR. WIESEL:

I do. Anti-Semitism is on the rise everywhere.

MR. PRESSMAN:

You lectured at the Sorbonne in Paris recently. Did you say there were bomb threats there?

MR. WIESEL:

Three—three bomb alerts at the Sorbonne, yes.

MR. PRESSMAN:

Just because you were lecturing?

MR. WIESEL:

Because I was there.

MR. PRESSMAN:

So you see it everywhere, all over the world.

MR. WIESEL:

I am afraid so. And our friend Cardinal Lustiger was there, and he knew about it. In my lifetime, I have seen anti-Semitism become a state religion in Germany. In my lifetime, I have seen anti-Semitism become a state ideology in the Soviet empire. In my lifetime, I have seen anti-Semitism dominate the Muslim world, although it's a contradiction in terms, but there anti-Semitism means anti-Jewishness.

MR. PRESSMAN:

When they say they're against the Zionist entity, you don't see that as a difference?

MR. WIESEL:

Oh, I'm afraid it means the same thing. It's a key word, a code, hiding something. Anti-Semitism, a French philosopher said, is the socialism of the imbeciles. It's easy. And what you say is true. Anti-Semites really believe that we dominate the world. I once had a dialogue on television with a great Catholic writer. And even he said, "Look, why are you so afraid? After all, you have so much power in New York and in Paris and in London." And I said, "Look, do you really believe that we control the world? We don't. But I am ready to make a deal with you. Give us the world for one generation. I promise you that when we give it back to you a generation later, it will be improved."

Now, today, because of the political situation between Israel and the Palestinians, which is a tragedy, as we all know, anti-Semitism is on the rise. Now they have an added reason to hate Jews. "Look, these Jews are causing pain to other people." So I am concerned, very much so. Anti-Semitism is irrational: I am hated because I am a believer, and I am hated because I am a nonbeliever. I am hated because I am a capitalist. I am hated because I'm an anticapitalist.

I am hated because I am too nationalistic. And I am hated because I am cosmopolitan. If there is one area where all contradictions meet, it is anti-Semitism. They hate us for everything.

CARDINAL O'CONNOR:

I can't speak too freely about areas outside New York, but in regard to what has been happening in Israel and with the Palestinians, I think that there has been a certain diminishing—not a complete loss—of support for Israel in New York. Maybe that's not even accurate. Perhaps it's better to say there's been a *questioning* of Israel that hadn't existed previously.

But I haven't found any signs of this being translated into personal anti-Semitism. As part of a Catholic-Jewish dialogue, I met recently with a group of rabbis and representatives of some of the very active Jewish associations, not only from New York but from different parts of the country. We talked very frankly and always very sympathetically about the current situation in Israel.

It is widely known that while in Israel, on the Gaza Strip, and then upon returning from Israel, I pleaded publicly that unless there are solutions to the Palestinian situation, unless we recognize the horrors of the refugee camps, then there will never be peace in the Middle East. At the same time, I talked about the critical importance of the integrity and the security of Israel. And in this discussion that we had, we furthered that kind of dialogue. A number of Jewish representatives present were very much worried about this "new image" of Israel as an aggressor against Palestinians, because of what we have seen on television.

But I didn't get the impression that they were fearful that anti-Semitism itself was rising from this. Your experience is different, though.

21

MR. WIESEL:

My impression is that more swastikas are being painted on more synagogues. I personally receive more hate mail than before. And the hate mail is a response to my love for Israel.

CARDINAL O'CONNOR:

Is it a case of damned if you do, damned if you don't? Some people seem to use Israel as the rationalization for the anti-Semitism that exists in their hearts. But even if Israel were not used as the rationalization, some people would find some other way to justify their anti-Semitism.

MR. WIESEL:

I'm sure they could find other reasons to hate me without Israel. They don't need reasons, they invent their own reasons.

MR. PRESSMAN:

We see an increase in swastikas and vandalism as we approach every anniversary of Kristallnacht. The question of peace between Arab and Jew in the Holy Land, is it attainable now?

CARDINAL O'CONNOR:

Oh, I think it's attainable. For centuries Arabs and Jews have lived together in peace, in friendship. And there are places in the Middle East right now where that is the case. Is it attainable again? I don't think we can even afford to ask the question that way. We have to achieve peace in the Middle East.

MR. PRESSMAN:

You understand why the prime minister of Israel and certain other Israeli politicians don't trust the PLO and their promise to coexist with Israel?

CARDINAL O'CONNOR:

Oh, I think I could understand anything of that sort. I won't enter into a discussion of it because I've certainly never talked with a prime minister of Israel about it and I've never talked with Mr. Arafat. But I think you have to transcend both when you talk about Palestinians. I think it's most unfortunate that there is an image of Palestinians and Arabs in the United States as all being guerrillas and terrorists.

I am president of the Catholic Near East Welfare Association. We have humanitarian activities in some eighteen countries in the Middle East, including Israel. During my travels on behalf of CNEWA, I have personally met with many people of these countries and the goodness and good will of the vast majority of them is clear.

I am also involved in a unique program which is run at the Kennedy School of Government at Harvard University. This program has already brought to the United States a number of college graduates from Israel, Jordan and Egypt with the permission of those governments. Our idea in bringing them together and asking them to live together, study together and work together and get certified at Kennedy School of Government is that they will go back and work together and try to establish, for example, public health clinics and do other hands-on humanitarian activities. I interviewed two of the students recently. One is an Arab Christian, the other a Jew. Both women were born in

23

Jerusalem. They are now working together very closely and are planning to open a clinic together when they go back. So it is possible. I believe it is essential.

MR. PRESSMAN:

What do you see?

MR. WIESEL:

I feel the same urgency. Something must be done. Forty years represents one biblical generation and that's too long for this tension to go on. To answer your specific question, I understand Israeli hesitation. After all, the Palestinians had a chance. They had more than one chance to establish a state in '47 if they had accepted the partition plan. Lydda would not be Israel today. Naharia would not be Israel today. Jerusalem would not be Israel today. Then between '48 and '67, the Palestinians had a chance of establishing a Palestinian state in the territories. Why didn't they? The truth is nobody thought about it. Nobody cared about the Palestinians. So I feel for the young Palestinians who feel betrayed by the whole world, not only by the Jewish people and by Israel. They *were* betrayed. But on the other hand, I cannot forget that the intention of the Arab states in '48 was to wipe out Israel. In '67, they again wanted to wipe out Israel. And Israel cannot afford a single defeat. If Israel is defeated once, it's the end of Israel. So I can understand the Israelis' worries and skepticism. And yet I am confident that Shamir will be more moderate than many people believe. Why? Remember ten years ago or so, it was Camp David. Begin was a hardliner. He gave up to Sadat more than Sadat had expected. Sadat was surprised when he received the whole of Sinai. And if Begin did it with Sadat,

24

then I'm sure Shamir could do many things that would surprise the world.

CARDINAL O'CONNOR:

Don't misunderstand. I don't fault Israel for being very cautious and very anxious about what might happen. The question was about specific people, about Shamir and Arafat. I think it would be inappropriate for me to calculate how either should address the other. But I'm in total sympathy with Israel's concern about what could happen. I think that the world at large could help by issuing as close to absolute guarantees as can be granted in this imperfect world about the security of Israel, the future of Israel. And I would add: the security and dignity of Palestinians.

MR. PRESSMAN:

But is it possible to sit down with the enemy who has wanted to kill you? Here's a little state the size of New Jersey that's been surrounded by a hundred million Arabs whose leaders have for forty years—

CARDINAL O'CONNOR:

In every war, you must sit down with your enemies. We sat down with the Japanese, for example.

MR. WIESEL:

After you defeated them.

CARDINAL O'CONNOR:

After we defeated them, yes.

MR. WIESEL:

Sure, you sat down with the Japanese and the Germans after you defeated them. You dictated your terms. But I'll tell you why I'm optimistic. Sadat arrived in Jerusalem on a Saturday night. Here in the U.S. it was still Sabbath. And I turned on the television, which I usually don't do on the Sabbath. I had to see. I was very moved by Sadat. I watched history at its best; an exalted moment of destiny. And I cried. But I didn't only cry because of Sadat. I was moved by the way he was received by my brothers and sisters in Israel. These same Israelis who, three or four years earlier, had suffered because of Sadat, received him with open arms. There were many orphans, many widows in the crowd, women who lost their husbands, their sons, their brothers in a war that Sadat had unleashed on the eve of Yom Kippur in '73. And yet it was enough for Sadat to come to Jerusalem on that Saturday evening—that Sabbath evening—for the people to undergo a real metamorphosis.

MR. PRESSMAN:

I was—

MR. WIESEL:

You were there.

MR. PRESSMAN:

I was with a family in Jerusalem watching their television set and they cried.

26

From left, Mr. Wiesel, Cardinal O'Connor, and Mr. Pressman, during the taping of the WNBC-TV broadcast, "A Journey of Faith," at St. Joseph's Seminary in Yonkers, New York. *(Courtesy WNBC-TV)*

President Reagan awards a congressional gold medal to Mr. Wiesel. *(UPI/ Bettmann Newsphotos)*

At the same ceremony, Mr. Wiesel urges President Reagan to cancel his visit to the cemetery near Bitburg, Germany, that contains the graves of S.S. soldiers. "What people don't know is that actually I had sent my speech to the President a day before." *(UPI/Bettmann Newsphotos)*

Mr. Wiesel again asks the President to cancel his trip to Bitburg, here at a lecture to a group in Philadelphia a few days later. Cardinal O'Connor also asked the President to reconsider his trip. *(UPI/ Bettmann Newsphotos)*

Catholic Chaplain Cdr. John J. O'Connor says Mass in a field near DaNang, March, 1965. "This picture of Vietnam recalls sad days." *(UPI/Bettmann Newsphotos)*

Chaplain O'Connor offers Communion to a U.S. Marine during a memorial service in the field near DaNang. "There's an air of unreality to me about the time this photograph recalls." *(UPI/Bettmann Newsphotos)*

Inmates at Buchenwald Concentration Camp, when U.S.
troops arrived, April, 1945. The face on the far right of
the center bunk is Elie Wiesel's. Mr. Pressman: "I find it
difficult to give you these pictures." *(UPI/Bettmann
Newsphotos)*

Photograph of Auschwitz taken accidentally by an Air Force photographer surveying bombing damage to factories near the camp. *(UPI/Bettmann Newsphotos)*

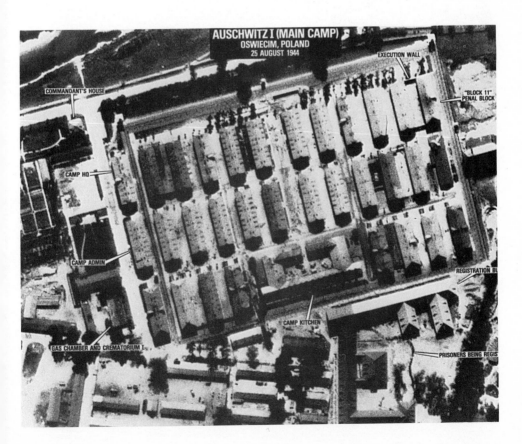

Mothers with children climb out of a freight wagon that brought them to Auschwitz, Poland. Mr. Wiesel: "They [the children] were the first to go. Why were they the first? Somehow it was as if the killers and the children couldn't co-exist under the same sky." *(UPI/Bettmann Newsphotos)*

Cardinal O'Connor prays at Jerusalem's Western Wall, 1987. "All I've thought and prayed...just flooded through me as I prayed at the Wall." *(UPI/Bettmann Newsphotos)*

During his installation as Archbishop of New York, Cardinal O'Connor places his mitre on the head of his namesake, John Joseph O'Connor (no relation), a boy who had written to congratulate him on his appointment. "That was another one of those completely spontaneous things....It was a moment of indescribable joy." *(UPI/ Bettmann Newsphotos)*

Mr. Wiesel responds to a question during a press conference following the announcement that he was awarded the Nobel Peace Prize, 1986. *(UPI/Bettmann Newsphotos)*

Mr. Wiesel with his wife at right, with Lech Walesa, during a visit to the Nazi death camp Auschwitz-Birkenau, Poland, on the 43rd anniversary of the evacuation of the camp, 1988. *(UPI/Bettmann Newsphotos)*

Mr. Wiesel and Cardinal O'Connor. *(Courtesy WNBC-TV)*

MR. WIESEL:

I was so moved when I saw the people, thousands of people receiving him as a brother. That means that hope is possible.

CARDINAL O'CONNOR:

Here's where I see the great grace of God. I think that Sadat transcended himself as did the Jewish people. I suspect that when Sadat started this journey, he wasn't at all sure he was going to go as far as he went. And I think that God lifted him up out of himself and I think that the reception that he was given in Israel was a kind of lifting up by God. God is the ultimate peace.

MR. WIESEL:

I invited his daughter, Camilla Sadat, she's at Boston University, to a recent seminar on hatred and the anatomy of hatred. She told me she was with her father throughout the time he prepared for the trip. And that he, too, was in a different state of mind. She says that he knew he was going to be killed.

MR. PRESSMAN:

The anatomy of hatred?

MR. WIESEL:

Yes.

MR. PRESSMAN:

Isn't that what this is all about?

MR. WIESEL:

It is what it's essentially all about. Hatred. Racial hatred. Political hatred. Ideological hatred. Religious hatred. This is the century of hatred and therefore I believe we must dissect it, we must face it, explore it, disarm it. And maybe then we have a chance.

MR. PRESSMAN:

You said once, I think, that the opposite of hatred is not love, it's indifference.

MR. WIESEL:

I believe that. Hatred becomes powerful only in the context of indifference. What was Nazism? Nazism was anti-Semitism in power. Before that—anti-Semites shouted, screamed, yelled. But it is only when the activities of anti-Semites and bigots are law that you have such things as apartheid. And the only way to fight bigotry and racism is to unmask it, to speak up, to not be indifferent. More words, but what else do we have? I have nothing else.

CARDINAL O'CONNOR:

"All power corrupts. Absolute power corrupts absolutely." However, I certainly wouldn't call indifference the *opposite* of hatred. I think there's a matter of definitions here. You say that within indifference hatred gains ascendancy, but I think the opposite of hatred is love, still.

MR. WIESEL:

Well, to quote myself correctly, what I said was, "The opposite of love is not hatred but indifference."

CARDINAL O'CONNOR:

Ah, you're right. In Scripture we read, "I know your deeds; I know you are neither hot nor cold. How I wish you were one or the other—hot or cold! But because you are luke-warm, neither hot nor cold, I will spew you out of my mouth!" (Revelation 3:15–16).

MR. PRESSMAN:

Going back to Sadat, do you both think that Shamir and the Israeli government should invite Arafat to come to Jerusalem now, or soon?

MR. WIESEL:

I think it would be a clever move on Israel's part or rather, it would have been a clever move a while ago. Now, it seems difficult because it would appear as though it were dictated by the events. If they had invited Arafat to Jerusalem it would have been a great coup, at least in terms of public relations. But we are not dealing here with public relations. We are dealing with—with destiny. That's why the situation is so serious. We are dealing first of all with the lives of hundreds and thousands of children and we cannot but feel empathy and sorrow for these children on both sides. And then we are dealing with the destiny of two peoples.

MR. PRESSMAN:

Hasn't the PLO been very successful in winning a great public relations victory over the state of Israel?

MR. WIESEL:

They have, yes. They have won and I, by the way, agree that a major step was taken when Arafat denounced terrorism.

Words are important. And when Arafat in Strasbourg and then in Geneva said that he recognizes the state of Israel, that was very important. I would like to see him go one step further, two steps further. I would like him first of all to abrogate the covenant. Because the PLO covenant still stipulates the destruction of Israel and says they must use every means at their disposal to bring about the destruction of Israel. Second, since he is the leader of the PLO and therefore the leader of the Palestinians, I would like him to proclaim a cease-fire in the territories. No peace has ever been attained without a cease-fire. He should say, all right, for six months there will be a cease-fire, no stone-throwing, no Molotov cocktail attacks. Let's allow the situation to calm down and then Israel and Palestine will speak. I think if he wants us to believe in his leadership that is what he should do.

CARDINAL O'CONNOR:

What I am about to ask is not your favorite subject—

MR. WIESEL:

No?

CARDINAL O'CONNOR:

Pope John Paul II was bitterly criticized when he received Arafat. I have never seen published what he said to Arafat. Interestingly, when I was in a meeting with Jews and Catholics a few weeks ago, some of the knowledgeable Jewish representatives were aware of this and read the statement that the Pope talked very firmly to Arafat about denouncing terrorism and about friendship toward Israel, and about rescinding terrorism against Israel. This came from Pope John Paul II.

MR. WIESEL:

Eminence, I like you too much, and we are good friends. I don't like to disagree with you publicly, but my view on the Pope is somewhat—

CARDINAL O'CONNOR:

I know, and that's why I brought it up.

MR. WIESEL:

Then let's talk about it. I am not sure that he should have seen Arafat. In fact, I think he should not have seen Arafat because he gave him a legitimacy which Arafat, at least at that time, did not deserve. Nor do I think that the Pope should have seen Waldheim twice, once in Austria and once in Rome. But you know, I have so many questions. We don't disagree often, but on these points we disagree.

MR. PRESSMAN:

You talked a moment ago, Mr. Wiesel, about the Pope receiving Waldheim. Didn't the Pope have to receive him as a head of state of a Roman Catholic country?

MR. WIESEL:

For me to say painful things about other people is difficult. It's not my style. If I cannot praise, I usually keep quiet. And even about the Pope, I only spoke out once because it hurt. It had to do with Waldheim. No, there was no reason

31

for the Pope to receive Waldheim even if Waldheim asked, and I know he asked. I think the Pope could have waited to receive him. Secondly, I was upset by the warmth with which the Pope received him—but then the Pope is probably a very warm man. He receives everybody like that. But I'm sure he must have known the pain he would cause to many Jews. He knew. For the Pope is also a man of the world.

CARDINAL O'CONNOR:

Judgment, judgment, always matters of judgment. I'm not speaking of the judgments of criticism. It is unlike the Jewish mind to condemn without a trial. Waldheim had had a trial before world opinion, but he hadn't had a formal trial. Without that, what reasons could the Pope have given for not seeing him? Once again, what did the Pope say in private? This is probably a matter that you and I will never be able to resolve, because it's a matter of judgment.

I have been accused of such excessive loyalty to this Pope that I cannot conceive of his being wrong about anything. That's foolish. He's a human being, infallible only within the most severely restricted circumstances, and certainly not when merely expressing opinions or making ordinary human judgments. Some who disagreed with him concerning the Waldheim visit, for example, were disappointed that I didn't denounce him. That "failure" was construed as evidence of my "blind loyalty." The fact is that the Pope exercised his judgment, I exercised mine, the critics exercised theirs. My judgment was rooted in neither blindness nor loyalty, but in circumstances quite unrelated to either.

As I see the Pope, he attempts always to take the long-range view, regardless of whatever storms of criticism may burst upon him during the immediate set of circumstances. What will a certain thing accomplish six months from now, a year from now, three years from now? The difficulty in talking about this is that a question is asked that you really can't answer appropriately: "Would *you* have done this? Do *you* think that the Pope should have received him?"

I can only say that there's no question in my mind that the Pope did what he thought he should do.

MR. WIESEL:

Why, I'm sure of that. But we know what he said to him, because there was a public ceremony. In public, the Pope seemed to praise him. He praised him for his works of peace . . .

CARDINAL O'CONNOR:

But we don't know what was said to him privately.

MR. PRESSMAN:

Let's consider another Pope that some Jewish historians and leaders have criticized strongly for not doing enough to protect or help the Jews of Europe in World War II, Pius XII. You feel strongly about that?

MR. WIESEL:

I do. I do. But again, that should not be construed to mean that I'm against all popes. I have a profound respect for John XXIII. A very great man, a just man, a righteous of the righteous. But I'm afraid that in the case of Pius, too, the Cardinal and I don't agree, because I feel that Pope Pius XII did not do enough.

I hear occasionally that there are documents in the Vatican that show otherwise, but they have not been made public. Maybe if I were to see those documents, I would change my mind. I have probably read everything that has been written on the subject. And I'm afraid my conclusion is that Pope Pius did not do all he could have to help the Jews during World War II.

CARDINAL O'CONNOR:

It is again a matter of judgment.

MR. WIESEL:

Sure, judgment. Sure.

CARDINAL O'CONNOR:

And I don't think all of the cards have been placed on the table. I agree with you that conceivably there are documents that haven't yet been made public, that have to be analyzed. What's the reason for not having done so? I don't know. But again, it's always a matter of human judgment.

MR. WIESEL:

Eminence, if the Pope had sent instructions to all the bishops and all the priests of all the cities and all the villages: Help the Jews—I'm sure that you agree with me that many Jews would have been saved. Such instructions were not sent.

CARDINAL O'CONNOR:

Yes, but I don't know why they weren't sent. And you don't know why they weren't sent.

34

MR. WIESEL:

I don't know, no.

CARDINAL O'CONNOR:

I do know that the American bishops made some very, very strong statements at the time.

MR. WIESEL:

If the Pope had sent instructions—after all, in the small villages of Eastern Europe, the respect for the Pope, the love of the Pope, the standing of the Pope were such that if the people had received the word: We must help Jews— many, I don't know how many, but many would have been helped.

CARDINAL O'CONNOR:

That's a judgment. My readings show, for instance, that the Pope was responsible for saving some 850,000 Jews. Out of six million, could more have been saved? Would more damage have been done? It's a matter of judgment. What would a man like myself do? What I would do wouldn't necessarily be the right thing to do. I am afraid that I have demonstrated over the course of five years in New York that I'm capable of saying things that shouldn't be said, that ultimately may do more harm than good.

MR. WIESEL:

That's why we're friends.

MR. PRESSMAN:

You shoot from the ecclesiastical hip?

CARDINAL O'CONNOR:

The ecclesiastical hip? I don't think so. Maybe from the ecclesiastical heart. And Pascal says the heart has its reasons that reason never knows, but that doesn't make it wise or prudent. It may make it very sincere. It may not necessarily be the right judgment. History will have to determine what Pope Pius XII did. I don't think there's been enough study yet.

MR. WIESEL:

Let me ask you just one question about the differences between Catholics and Jews. After all, I am a Jew and you are a devout Catholic. I try to be a pretty good Jew. In the Jewish tradition, we may say anything about anyone, except God well, even God, to God, about God—but what the Talmud says about Moses or the Talmud says about our great prophets is totally iconoclastic.

I personally, for instance, in years past, have often voiced sadness over the behavior of certain American Jewish leaders. They didn't do enough. But if someone asked you if you believe that the Pope was wrong, would you say so if you did?

CARDINAL O'CONNOR:

Yes, I would if I came into possession of sufficient evidence to make me think that he had made a bad judgment. Because it was a human judgment. And I have the freedom to criticize a Pope's human judgment.

36

Rabbi Lookstein has done a great service, I think, in his book on the silence of the American Jews during the Holocaust, *Were We Our Brother's Keepers?*

MR. WIESEL:

I prefaced it.

CARDINAL O'CONNOR:

Of course. When my friend Arthur Goldberg, former justice of the Supreme Court, joined a commission to study the behavior of American Jews during the war, he felt that too much was being covered up and so he quit, out of integrity. Would I be interested in joining a study of people's response to the war? Yes. I have publicly invited others to join with me in trying to sponsor a joint study. It's very difficult for even a meticulously scholarly Jewish researcher or a meticulously scholarly Catholic researcher, working alone, without the perspective of the other.

MR. PRESSMAN:

This study would be just on this question?

MR. WIESEL:

Let's do it. If you give us access to all the documents in the Vatican pertaining to this period, then let's do it. Together—I'm ready to do it together with you.

CARDINAL O'CONNOR:

Well, obviously all I can do is request that these be made available; I can't . . .

MR. WIESEL:

Request, request the opening of the archives.

CARDINAL O'CONNOR:

Yes.

MR. WIESEL:

And then you and I establish a joint commission of Jewish and Catholic scholars.

CARDINAL O'CONNOR:

I think it would be a great contribution to the world. It's fascinating that prior to 1963—when Hochhuth wrote his play, *The Deputy*—there seemed to be very, very little questioning.

MR. WIESEL:

No, there was.

CARDINAL O'CONNOR:

Well, at least a lot of good things were being said about Pius XII. You admit that?

MR. WIESEL:

The first to write against the Pope was a Catholic writer, François Mauriac. Before Hochhuth.

CARDINAL O'CONNOR:

But the first to publicize it, so that it came to wide public attention, was Hochhuth in the play *The Deputy*.

MR. WIESEL:

Well, it was, of course, a sensational play.

CARDINAL O'CONNOR:

And from that point on, there has been confusion, conster-
nation, feelings of guilt and embarrassment, feelings of
resentment on the part of Catholics who passionately defend Pius XII.

MR. PRESSMAN:

Catholic-Jewish relations in America—what do you think
of the state of those relations now, Mr. Wiesel?

MR. WIESEL:

I think there are ups and downs. I am not really familiar
with the subject, I'm not involved in it. I don't represent
anybody. I'm the president of no organization, the chairman of no group. I'm totally alone. And I can tell you that
when I meet the Cardinal, and I have a few other friends
in the Church, I feel that we are making headway. We are
open and honest. I am a Jew. And I try out of my Jewish-
ness to help other people understand my religion and their
own.

And I expect the same from the Cardinal. I have total
respect for the Cardinal as a Christian. Jews never believed
that it was our duty to turn the whole world Jewish. Our
mission was to make the world more hospitable. Even if
the Messiah comes, there would still be many people,
many religions—except the world would be more tolerant
and more hospitable.

And I think that whenever the Cardinal and I meet,
there's always a step forward.

CARDINAL O'CONNOR:

Much progress is being made. The fact that we sit and talk, those of us in the so-called dialogue, is tremendously helpful. The Pope himself met with a group of Jewish representatives who questioned him very, very freely; he answered very freely.

But no matter how hard we try, we inevitably come to a halt on a particular question: Why hasn't the Holy See extended formal diplomatic recognition to Israel?

A lot of people will say why should this be involved in a theological discussion? The answer is we believed for many years that the Church had theological objections to formal diplomatic recognition of Israel. The Pope has removed that. The Pope has stated categorically that there are no theological obstacles.

I see Israel as perhaps some Jews don't. I see Israel as the embodiment of everything that is Judaism, everything that is Jews, everything that Israel has meant through history, that God has kept alive, that God has sustained. The Shekinah has gone before, if you will, the cloud by day and the pillar of fire by night. And now Israel is led back to this geographical location. To me, the Church has done something almost infinitely beyond recognizing territorial boundaries.

But recognizing the reality of Israel is to recognize the reality of a mystery that I don't think even many Jews pretend to understand. I don't think you pretend to understand the mystery of it.

MR. WIESEL:

I don't.

The existence of Israel to me is mystery. Who would

have expected it? What my grandfather saw as a dream, as a prayer, is now reality.

CARDINAL O'CONNOR:

"Next year in Jerusalem."

MR. WIESEL:

It isn't only that. It is much more than that. A sovereign state. On its very land, the very land of its ancestors. It's extraordinary. I don't understand it. But still, I would like the Pope to recognize Israel, because we live in a world where gestures are important.

MR. PRESSMAN:

Can it happen, Your Eminence, in this Pope's lifetime?

CARDINAL O'CONNOR:

Well, I've recently written a book where I address this. The problems are still being discussed. Some of those problems are the status of Jerusalem, which is in part a question of free access to Jerusalem, to the holy places of Jerusalem; the ultimate resolution of the Palestinian situation, if I can call it such; and security for Christians throughout the Middle East. Some may not think each is a legitimate question. The Pope does. I do.

If these questions can be rationally resolved, then it would be difficult to see any obstacle to formal diplomatic recognition of Israel. But I think there's a potential beyond that, although this is purely my own personal speculation. The Pope represents a spiritual entity. Granted, he's the head of a "sovereign state," and has a little piece of territory to safeguard this. But what would the Pope be if that were it, if all he had was Vatican City? The Pope is the spiritual representative of a world body that we believe to be a spiritual mystery—Roman Catholicism.

His status, his spiritual power, is intertwined in his being the personification of this mystery of Catholicism. To me, Israel is the personification of the mystery of Judaism. I'm clearly not a diplomat, and I'm not diplomatically in the employ of the Holy See. But I would see a tremendous potential in a formal recognition between two spiritual entities which might serve as a prelude to formal diplomatic relations.

MR. PRESSMAN:

Do you feel that you'd like to see the Vatican consider some kind of spiritual recognition of Israel? I don't quite understand that.

CARDINAL O'CONNOR:

I don't understand it either. I'm talking mystery, so I won't pretend to understand mystery.

MR. WIESEL:

Don't talk mystery to journalists. [*Laughter*]

CARDINAL O'CONNOR:

Again, I'm not a diplomat, I'm not formally engaged in diplomatic affairs. I have no official status to represent the Holy See in such matters. But I think that this is *an* approach, beginning with a clearer articulation of what the Pope is, who the Pope is, and a clearer articulation of what Israel is.

MR. PRESSMAN:

Could you see the Pope, could you see the Vatican, Mr. Wiesel, as a catalyst for peace in the Middle East?

MR. WIESEL:

For the moment, how could the Vatican be that? The Vatican doesn't even recognize Israel. I think the Vatican should recognize Israel. I'll tell you why. Maybe it wouldn't do much—one more country recognizing Israel. But the absence of recognition has a certain negative symbolic value.

CARDINAL O'CONNOR:

Yes, I think it's much more than one more country recognizing another.

MR. WIESEL:

Exactly. Therefore, I think the Vatican should recognize Israel. Till then, there is no way! Why should Israel listen to the Vatican, if there is no recognition?

MR. PRESSMAN:

Not a spiritual recognition. That's not enough for you?

MR. WIESEL:

No, that's not enough for me. Because it's a symbol—

CARDINAL O'CONNOR:

But you must do things incrementally.

MR. WIESEL:

Forty years! We are waiting forty years. The march in the desert is over.

CARDINAL O'CONNOR:

It should be noted that until very recently, there were no formal diplomatic relations between the Holy See and the United States. Yet during World War II the Holy See was able to carry out many services for the United States. Indeed, the Holy Father is personally viewed by many nations of varying religious postures as a major figure in helping nations to avoid war or to reconcile disputes.

And you'd be the last one in the world to say that because we've waited forty years, there's no point in trying anything further.

MR. WIESEL:

Of course.

MR. PRESSMAN:

In a turbulent world, the question of who is a Jew, who is a Catholic looms larger than ever. Are you concerned about slippage, about losing the identity of a people?

MR. WIESEL:

Of course I'm concerned. But the debate, the storm that swept through Jewish communities a while ago about the question who is a Jew I think was wrong. It was ill-conceived, ill-timed and unnecessary. For two thousand years we lived without it. A Jew is someone who links his or her destiny to the destiny of the Jewish people. And it is that

44

linkage, that fusion of memory, the individual one and the collective one, that gives the identity to the individual and then to the people. The loss of that memory would be the loss of that identity.

MR. PRESSMAN:

Are you concerned that that may be happening, that assimilation may be destroying that identity?

MR. WIESEL:

I'm concerned, naturally, because I've lost too many people. We lost so many. And to lose one more, even one, hurts our people. But then, I must confess to you, I don't see so many assimilated Jews. The Jews who come to my lectures are Jews who are committed to Judaism and, I believe, to humanity. And I feel sorry for those who are assimilated, who give up such treasures, who give up such a past. After all, my tradition tells me that I am directly linked to Moses and to Rabbi Akiba. And that whatever I say now, Moses has already heard from God at Sinai. For this is what we believe. And for the artist, for the musician, for the thinker, for the teacher to give up such treasures—does he or she realize the magnitude of the loss that he or she endures?

MR. PRESSMAN:

Are the Jewish people losing out? Do you think that there is attrition—significant, serious attrition?

MR. WIESEL:

In the newspapers I read that there are losses. But we've always been a small people. And I am not pessimistic. As long as we have good teachers, we shall manage to convey the beauty of our tradition. Not only the truth of our tradition, because we share this truth with everybody else, but the beauty of it as well. The beauty for the Jew to be Jewish is, I believe, the same as the beauty for the Christian to be Christian. I've tried to teach that for the last thirty, forty years.

MR. PRESSMAN:

Are you concerned, Your Eminence, about the alienation from your faith of many Catholics right now?

CARDINAL O'CONNOR:

I would say in almost the words of Elie Wiesel, of course I'm concerned. If I believe what I believe, if I believe in the beauty and the depth and the richness of Catholicism, if I believe that the Catholic faith is the guardian, the custodian of truth, not necessarily purporting to understand all of the truth—but if I believe that people's lives can be enriched, that the gospel is the good news, then of course I'm concerned if people turn away from it. If you're cold and you turn away from the fire, you're going to get colder. If you're hungry and you turn away from food, you're going to get more hungry and then starve, and this concerns me very much. It doesn't concern me in terms of the size of Catholicism, aside from the Church. I agree with Professor Wiesel, the Church—although some people think it's so powerful and so huge, almost monstrous—the Church remains a minority in the world. So that it's not a matter of safeguarding numbers as such.

I think if one is a true Catholic, one has to be concerned about those who lose the faith, because their lives are diminished. We have a very special teaching, of course,

46

which is of equal importance. We believe that the Church is the body of Christ in the world. It's again a very mystical teaching. Each one of us is an eye or ear, or other organ. In that sense, the body of Christ cannot afford to lose anyone. Every person is of tremendous importance. You, Professor Wiesel, don't want to lose one from Judaism. We don't want to lose one from the body of Christ, because we believe that the resurrection of Christ that took place physically on Easter Sunday is not completed until the whole body of Christ is filled up. It's a continuing thing. And if one is lost, some of the body of Christ is diminished. It has to be worrisome; it has to be a cause of anguish to anyone who is formally tasked with the responsibility to try to preserve the body of Christ intact and enhance it, rather than see it diminished.

MR. PRESSMAN:

Why have so many Catholics turned away from Church teachings, such as divorce or other matters?

CARDINAL O'CONNOR:

We're again dependent on polls, aren't we? Professor Wiesel said that he had read the newspaper to the effect that a number of Jews have left Judaism. I've read some of those same newspapers that tell me that there's an increased interest in Judaism, a fascinating interest in Judaism. While we say that a number of Catholics have turned away because of some of the teachings, turning away and not practicing, I think, are two different things. Formally rejecting in your heart is different from pretense or not practicing in your behavior. We're all weak. We're weak human beings. If I am a married man and my wife is a drunkard, or she leaves me, and I try to lead a celibate life, and then I'm tempted, and I want to get married again, and the Church says I can't get married, in human weakness, I'm possibly going to get married. And then I'm not practicing my faith. That doesn't mean that I have rejected Catholicism. The Church does not exist because people don't sin, but because they do sin. To blame the flood on Noah's ark is to blame all of the defections on the Church or Church teaching. Now, we must be much more understanding than that, that people drift, people at a given period in their lives reject teaching because it's very difficult to practice it.

MR. PRESSMAN:

Looking back on your lives, what person would you say had the greatest influence on you, going back to your childhood?

MR. WIESEL:

I have a few. First of all, my father, naturally; my mother. My grandfather. And my teacher of mysticism who was mad in the best and noblest sense of the word. And since then I have been fond of madmen. But of course, my grandfather, he's the one who with my mother brought me to Hasidism. And my father, he lived for other people. He taught me that until I see the other, I cannot be I. He had a grocery store. But most of his life was devoted to helping other people. Whenever anyone needed anything, refugees who needed papers, or someone was in jail, they came to my father. He had no official function in the town. He was just known for helping. As a result, he was rarely at home. I used to see him only on the Sabbath. And the rest of the week he would go around taking people out of jail. Then, during the war, he was arrested because he had obtained false papers for refugees from Poland and one of them was arrested. The authorities found my father's name. And I know that he was tortured. But he never spoke about it. And only during the war, when we were together in Auschwitz, did we really became close. Because then I had him and he had me. And those months were very, very special. And until he—while he was alive, I had a desire to live. When he died, I felt that I had stopped living. Between the end of January and April '45, I wasn't alive. But during the war, we became so close—because we were together literally twenty-four hours a day. And I felt I had to be alive simply to keep him alive, to give him a reason to go on living. And he felt probably the same thing. So it is my father, of course, who gave me an example and a lesson. And of course, my mother, but I rarely speak of my mother because I'm always afraid I will cry. And then the teacher, an extraordinary teacher who taught me the beauty of mysticism, the beauty of trying to save the world with a few prayers, a few words. That's all. We say a few words and the world is saved. That is mysticism.

MR. PRESSMAN:

But he had a sense of humor, too, didn't he?

MR. WIESEL:

They all had a sense of humor. Sometimes a sense of humor was so special, so delicate, that you were afraid to smile in order to keep its reverberation in your memory and in your life intact.

MR. PRESSMAN:

Your father had a great influence on you, too, Your Eminence?

CARDINAL O'CONNOR:

Oh, yes. Oh, yes. I'm lost in some things that Elie Wiesel said here, and I want to comment on them. But I'm struck by the similarities, because my father overwhelmingly shaped my life. My mother certainly, and teachers were of crucial importance, too, and particular friends one meets along the way. The people who died in Dachau shaped my adult life. But my father—my father was an extraordinary man in that everyone was the same to him, literally. That's why I sometimes think I may be unique in history. This is a silly thing to say, though I'll say it anyway. I grew up with no conscious prejudices, because to my father, a human being was a person made in the image and likeness of God. And if he was prejudiced at all, it was against the wealthy. Not because he wasn't wealthy, but because he felt that we pay far too much attention to the wealthy. We treat the wealthy with great deference. And if you're told that some great person is coming to your house, then you turn the house inside out and upside down. But he would do that for a bricklayer, or a carpenter or a plumber, or a simple person, a street cleaner. He was an extraordinarily skilled man. He had hands with very long fingers, and they were very dexterous. He was a gold leafer; he did the ceilings of churches. And everything was very authentic.

MR. PRESSMAN:

He put the gold leaf on the ceilings?

CARDINAL O'CONNOR:

Yes. Did I ever tell you about that? Did you know how this was done? He was almost one of the last of the Mohicans. It was almost a lost art. Now, it's developing again. He would take me when I was a little kid to watch him leafing the ceiling of a church, the ceiling of a hotel, some of these old beautiful places where the gold would be very rich and would shine even in the darkness. He had a very narrow brush. And it was very soft. It was the only really expensive thing that he owned. He would have his books of gold leaf in very thin sheets. They would be placed in the book on very thin sheets of tissue paper. And he would make his own sizing, as it was called. The sizing was made out of egg white and some other things. He would put this sizing on the spots on which he was to put the gold. He would take the brush and work it with the deftness of a magician. It was hard for the eye to follow. He had a full head of white hair. He'd just touch the tip of the brush to his hair with the greatest speed, and with the static electricity he generated, pick up a leaf of gold like lightning, and apply it. He was a very skilled craftsman. He was always a union man. He didn't have to be. He gave me a passionate conviction of the importance of collective bargaining and the rights of people to defend themselves. But above all, and I can tell you this very honestly, from my simplest days I was taught to look at a person as a person. Jew, Protestant, Catholic, Moslem, whatever, black, white, yellow, man, woman, child and not look at a person's pockets, not to look at how much money the person might have. So this was terribly important in shaping my life. I mentioned Dachau before. But I want to go back to it. Not because I'm talking with you, Professor Wiesel. And not because we've reflected on

51

the Holocaust. I had the usual amount of theological study, and some extra philosophical study and studies in clinical psychology. So I thought I knew something about the human person. And I know I did. It would be foolish to say I didn't know anything. I knew what my faith taught. I knew what psychologists taught.

But when I went to Dachau, that was an experience that almost literally changed my life. Not so much by the drama as by the dramatic, stark simplicity of it. You leave Munich and you go through this little town where there are still window boxes filled with roses. It is all so peaceful. And you can imagine that that's the way that it was while the horror was taking place. Then you come to this open field that looks like an athletic field surrounded by a cyclone fence. And you see how prosaic it was, the banality of it. That was a shock for me. But then the moment came when I first put my hand into one of those semicircular red brick ovens and felt on the floor of that oven the intermingled ashes of Jews and Christians, lay persons, clergy, men, women, children. I asked, "Good God, could human beings do this to human beings?" That had a dramatic effect, a radical effect on me. I will never forget it.

It made me frighteningly conscious of the Holocaust, but more, of the persecution and the injustices and the violence toward every human person.

I'd like to do something now, Professor Wiesel, but only if you let me. You talked about your father and you at Auschwitz, and you said you stopped living. I have with me your seminal work, *Night.* I would like to read from it. Is it all right if I do this?

MR. WIESEL:

Sure.

52

CARDINAL O'CONNOR:

I want to quote from it and ask you a question afterwards. It may be an unfair question, so I'll ask the question in advance and you can be reflecting. It seems to me that what you describe in this passage had an indescribable effect, not only on that period in your life when you temporarily stopped living, but that it has driven you ever since. You talk about the fact that your father had become ill. This is toward the conclusion of this little book.

And you say a week went by when your father was just burning with fever and pleading for water. And this is what was said to you:

> "This is your father, isn't it?" asked the head of the block.
> "Yes."
> "He's very ill."
> "The doctor won't do anything for him."
> "The doctor *can't* do anything for him now. And neither can you."
> He put his great hairy hand on my shoulder and added:
> "Listen to me, boy. Don't forget that you're in a concentration camp. Here, every man has to fight for himself and not think of anyone else, even his father. Here, there are no fathers, no brothers, no friends. Everyone lives and dies for himself alone. I'll give you a sound piece of advice—don't give your ration of bread and soup to your old father. There's nothing you can do for him. And you're killing yourself. Instead, you ought to be having his ration."
> I listened to him without interrupting. He was right, I thought in the most secret region of my heart, but I dared not admit it. It's too late to save your old father,

I said to myself. You ought to be having two rations of bread, two rations of soup . . .

Only a fraction of a second, but I felt guilty. I ran to find a little soup to give my father. But he did not want it. All he wanted was water . . .

I brought him some water. Then I left the block for roll call. But I turned around and came back again. I lay down on the top bunk. Invalids were allowed to stay in the block. So I would be an invalid myself. I would not leave my father.

There was silence all around now, broken only by groans. In front of the block, the SS were giving orders. An officer passed by the beds. My father begged me:

"My son, some water . . . I'm burning . . . My stomach . . ."

"Quiet, over there!" yelled the officer.

"Eliezer," went on my father, "some water . . ."

The officer came up to him and shouted at him to be quiet. But my father did not hear him. He went on calling me. The officer dealt him a violent blow on the head with his truncheon.

I did not move. I was afraid. My body was afraid of also receiving a blow.

Then my father made a rattling noise and it was my name: "Eliezer."

I could see that he was still breathing—spasmodically.

I did not move.

When I got down after roll call, I could see his lips trembling as he murmured something. Bending over him, I stayed gazing at him for over an hour, engraving into myself the picture of his blood-stained face, his shattered skull.

Then I had to go to bed. I climbed into my bunk,

above my father, who was still alive. It was January 28, 1945.

I awoke on January 29 at dawn. In my father's place lay another invalid. They must have taken him away before dawn and carried him to the crematory. He may still have been breathing.

There were no prayers at his grave. No candles were lit to his memory. His last word was my name. A summons to which I did not respond.

I came to love you when I read that. And I have been willing to live with even what I think, at times, are your unfair criticisms of Pope John Paul II, whom I love, and whom I see differently from the way you see him, because this was the key to your authenticity.

Is it asking too much to ask, has this scene driven you through the years?

MR. WIESEL:

It still does. When I write, I often feel that they are looking over my shoulder to read what I write. When you write like that, you'd better tell the truth. And that is always the case, when I write about the Bible or the Talmud. I feel—literally I feel—they are looking. "What are you doing with our lives?" they say to me. "What are you doing with our death?" they say to me.

And once the feeling was even stronger than that. It was of all things during the Nobel ceremony. And the chairman of the Nobel committee, a marvelous gentleman, and in the presence of the king and the Parliament and the diplomatic corps—he ended his address saying "When your father died, you were with him, and that was the darkest moment, the most tragic moment in your life. Now you are living a glorious moment, and your son is with you. And I want him to come up with you."

And of course he thus bridged the two, the two moments in my life with a few words—my father and my son—and I couldn't speak. They were all waiting for me to say something. I couldn't speak. I couldn't speak because I saw my father . . . You understand?

Once upon a time, literature was entertainment. Mine is not. I believe that my words today must carry a moment, my father's memory. Every single word I write must honor that memory.

MR. PRESSMAN:

You told me once about going back to your home in Romania.

MR. WIESEL:

Now it's Romania. When I left it was Hungary.

MR. PRESSMAN:

It was Transylvania.

MR. WIESEL:

Transylvania.

MR. PRESSMAN:

Memories of your father in Transylvania, and of your father [indicates Cardinal O'Connor] in Pennsylvania . . . Could you, could you remind me of that story?

MR. WIESEL:

Oh, I went back to my house in Hungary. I wanted to know what happened, really, and I was drawn back. We Jews are drawn to our past, to our origins, always. To David's kingdom, and to the time when God was still talking to his creatures and they were still listening and hearing. We Jews are obsessed with the past. And I wanted to go back.

And I did, twenty years later. I had a feeling that I was dreaming. Nothing was real. Because the town had not changed. Everything was the same. The railway station, the municipal park, my street, my home. Except the Jews weren't there.

And I felt that I . . . I was living a nightmare. I had a feeling that maybe the catastrophe didn't occur. And I wanted to go back to my house, and I wanted to see: maybe it didn't happen. Maybe the door will open and my father will come out and say, "What are you doing?" And the child that used to resemble me will come out and ask me, "What are you doing?"

Finally I went into my house. And nothing had changed. I remembered there was a stove. I remember the discussions we had at home whether or not to build that stove because we were poor. I thought we were wealthy, but we were not. What struck me during that visit was the poverty of the Jewish people in my town. They were so terribly poor.

So I was there, and I saw the stove. It hadn't changed. The table and the furniture—in the same place! This creak of the door opening was the same. And people lived there. Not my father or my mother or my sister—other people.

I wasn't angry at them. It wasn't their fault. But all of a sudden, I saw on the wall something that brought me back to reality. I am a Hasid. Anyway, I come from Hasidic Judaism and my whole upbringing . . . my melodies are Hasidic melodies. My prayers are Hasidic prayers. When I was seven or eight, the Rabbi of Vizhnitz, who was a kind compassionate man, came to my town. He sat me on his knee and examined me. That was the custom. I was the last child he examined. I loved him with passion and fervor.

I remember when he died, I took his picture and put it on the wall over my bed. Now . . . the nail was there, but not his picture! There was, I think, a picture of the Virgin Mary. And that hit me with excruciating pain. I left silently, and in a way I'm still there.

CARDINAL O'CONNOR:

You're a better man than I am. I have never been able to go home. We lived in a little house in Philadelphia.

MR. PRESSMAN:

A row house?

CARDINAL O'CONNOR:

A little row house, a very simple little place. I lived there all my life as a kid, grew up there. And when my father died, that was very difficult for me. He was an invalid for five years. He suffered terribly physically, but even more emotionally.

I know that you and I differ somewhat in our concepts of suffering. I believe in the tremendous potential of suffering that, joined with the crucifixion of Christ, can help save the world. This is what I meant when I said previously that the only answer I am able to give about the question of how I tolerate the terrible things I have seen happen in my lifetime is the mystery and the potential of suffering. My father believed in that, so he offered all of his sufferings in this house. And then he died, and that was a great, great loss.

But then two years later, my mother died, and it was as though I was suddenly orphaned, even though a full-grown man. The rug of life had been pulled out from under me. There was no past.

The very day I learned of her death, I went to the house. I went through it once. All the pictures that were there of my childhood, my family, were just overwhelming to me. I took one or two little items and left. And not only have I never gone back, whenever I've been in that area of Philadelphia, I've deliberately detoured, so that I wouldn't have to see the house.

MR. WIESEL:

I have in front of my desk a picture of my house. Since I began writing, I always face that house. I must know where I come from. Whatever I write, it's always there. That picture is there. It was taken by a TV man who was there once, thirty years ago. Yes, I want to remember where I come from.

CARDINAL O'CONNOR:

But see, I have double roots. I have two legs—one foot firmly planted in Catholicism, but then, as a Catholic, the other firmly planted in Judaism, as is Catholicism itself. So we have the same sense of tradition. I have two thousand years of tradition here—just immensely important to me, immensely important.

And then, beneath and beyond that, we believe we have all of the same heritage that you have. From which we would never want to cut ourselves off.

MR. PRESSMAN:

Let me show you some pictures, and tell me what it brings back to you as you look at it.

MR. WIESEL:

That's Bitburg. The Bitburg picture.

MR. PRESSMAN:

When you got the medal from President Reagan.

MR. WIESEL:

What people don't know is that actually I had sent my speech to the president a day before. I believe in courtesy and respect—I really do.

MR. PRESSMAN:

So he knew you were going to say that place is not your place.

MR. WIESEL:

Of course. I sent him the entire address beforehand. And I even said it to him on the day of the ceremony, and told his staff: "Look, there's still time, don't go and you'll become the hero of the day." I believe, by the way, that he did *not* want to go. But he listened to his advisers, and, you know, he always relied on them.

But it was some experience, you know, to try respectfully to argue a case with the president of the United States.

CARDINAL O'CONNOR:

You know what this picture says to me? I have received avalanches of hate mail since becoming the Archbishop of New York. One came when I said that I would give a little bit of money that I didn't need for scholarships for black children. I received an avalanche of mail from whites asking why I restricted the scholarships to blacks. That's very understandable to me. The other came when I sent a telegram to President Reagan, urging him to reconsider going to Bitburg. I was astonished at the mail that I got. And it wasn't, "Who are you, a churchman, interfering in political life?" That wasn't it in this issue. I've been accused of that, of course, in the past. It was explicitly that I had entered into this very volatile question about the visit at the cemetery where clearly the Jews of the world were going to feel that their memories were being desecrated.

MR. WIESEL:

But not only theirs, not only the Jews'. At that time the whole country was against the visit! Literally the whole country. But the president listened to his advisers and to Chancellor Kohl. I felt then as I always do, people looking over my shoulders. I have a responsibility to them. I am not only writing for the living; I also write for the dead. All the protests didn't help. The president did go.

MR. PRESSMAN:

Let me ask you about this picture, Your Eminence.

61

CARDINAL O'CONNOR:

Oh, my goodness. They were the days when I had a lot of hair and I had to have it cut that short. This picture of Vietnam recalls sad days indeed. I would have Mass on the hood of my little jeep. The jeep was the altar. That picture was taken near Danang, which was up toward the north, considerably north of Saigon. I was with the Third Marine Division at the time.

Professor Wiesel talked about the feeling of unreality when he went back to his house; there's an air of unreality to me about the time this photograph recalls. Those days seem so long ago, so many people who died, so much suffering.

MR. PRESSMAN:

You wrote, "No priest can ever watch the blood pouring from the wounds of the dying without anguish and a sense of desperate frustration and futility. Every war is the wrong war in the wrong place and at the wrong time."

CARDINAL O'CONNOR:

Yes. I remember writing those words, I think probably in my book on Vietnam, which I've said since wasn't a very good book. But it was an honest book; it was an effort to think through the morality and/or legality of the war in Vietnam. Not very many people were attempting to do that at the time.

I think I was wrong in much of what I thought. But I was right, I think, in much of what I thought. I recall when I was working on the pastoral letter on war and peace with bishops of the United States. I was certainly never a hero, but I had spent twenty-seven years in uniform with the Navy and the Marine Corps and knew a little bit about the war. I tried always to urge clarity of thought. Let's analyze the issues as carefully, as sensitively as we can, and let's not brush aside truth and reality in the interest simply of condemning war. It's easy to condemn war, but how do you prevent war? How do you preserve an innocent people from attack from an adversary?

To speak of total disarmament is a wonderful utopia. But meanwhile, how do you keep people from being destroyed by unjust aggressors? It's a very difficult thing. Well, I aroused the anger of a great number of people because I seemed to be indiscriminately defending war, as such. I never, never indiscriminately defended war as such, although I do believe that a given war can be a "just war." No priest could see blood pouring to the ground from human bodies and defend war as such indiscriminately. Every war is indeed the wrong war in the wrong place at the wrong time, but saying that doesn't rid the world of war, tragically.

MR. PRESSMAN:

I find it difficult to give you these pictures, but I wanted to know, when you looked at them, what your thoughts and feelings are now.

MR. WIESEL:

This one, I'll tell you how it came to be published. I was sitting with President Carter in the Oval Office, when he asked me to become chairman of what became the President's Commission on the Holocaust. But I didn't want to be a public figure; I am not good at these things. I like to teach and to study and to read and to write.

He insisted, and then he said to me, "You know, before you came, I asked Admiral Turner, Pat Turner, who was CIA director, to find in our archives what we have about the places you were in. As a gift for you. And he found these pictures. Now, what happened was the following: the Air Force bombed factories near Auschwitz, and of course they took pictures of the area before and after. By chance, the navigator forgot to shut the camera, and that that is how the camera took pictures of the camp.

So I sat with the president, and I became his guide, and I showed him what the pictures meant. They were clear, everything in them was clear. At the end, I asked him, "What would you have done, had you been president then?" And I must say that President Carter is an honest man. He said, "I don't know. I wish I could tell you I would have done the right thing." We were talking about Roosevelt and my problems with him, too.

This one, of course, is . . . I think of all the children, I am always at the edge of the abyss, when I am confronted by these children, one million or one-and-a-half million children. I don't know; it drives me to rage. Why? Why children? How could the world do that to children?

And yet they were the first to go. Why were they the first? Somehow it was as if the killers and the children couldn't co-exist under the same sky. And . . . to the end of my life, I will see those processions of children walking through the night, drawn into the flames.

MR. PRESSMAN:

"Never shall I forget that night, the first night in camp, which has turned my life into one long night."

MR. WIESEL:

I wrote it, in my book, and I would repeat it today. I stand behind every word.

MR. PRESSMAN:

Your Eminence?

CARDINAL O'CONNOR:

The Western Wall. Yes, I think that whatever is deep within me, all of my roots, all of the experience at Dachau, all I've thought and prayed since, just flooded through me as I prayed at that Wall. All of the current horrors out there and all of the pain and the suffering of the Palestinians and Jews overwhelmed me, knowing that I was in virtually an armed fortress, just being in Israel, and how people there have to live.

It also brings back a very sad memory for me, a memory of terrible misunderstanding. You were with me, Gabe. We went into Yad Vashem, the Holocaust museum.

MR. PRESSMAN:

It's when you came out and said that the suffering of the Jewish people was a great gift to mankind.

CARDINAL O'CONNOR:

Yes. And I said that within the context of my theology. I was utterly astonished at the resentment, the bitterness that this statement aroused. I "blamed" part of it on Elie Wiesel, because he writes so much about suffering, and I was in a mood of great suffering, feeling the sufferings of the Jewish people. This goes back to what I said before—

65

MR. PRESSMAN:

Well, I was there, and I saw your reaction and the reaction of your aide, Monsignor McCarthy, and you came out with your eyes full of tears and your face red. And when you said this in that context, it was clear that it came from your heart and from your theology.

CARDINAL O'CONNOR:

I don't think that it is unfair today to call the Holocaust central to the mystery of the Jewish faith. To me, the central mystery of all history is the crucifixion of Christ. To me, the crucifixion of Christ changed everything. To me, the crucifixion of Christ and all of the suffering in the crucifixion of Christ made possible the salvation of the world.

My father taught me to unite all suffering with the sufferings of the Christ on the cross. If my feet hurt, if I had a headache, if I'd been rebuffed or rejected, if my feelings were hurt, if somebody had laughed at me or ridiculed me, he urged me to unite it to the sufferings of Christ on the cross, and that it would bring down graces on people I would never see. I grew up believing that and believe it today with all my heart. This is what I was thinking when I made my remark at Yad Vashem, that no suffering of a people, no suffering of humanity, has ever been what the Holocaust was. And I saw tremendous healing potential in their suffering.

If one's theology is different, one looks at it differently. I've read all that you've said about suffering. I recently quoted your work, *Against Silence.* You say that when the Messiah comes, he will go around and catch the tears of all Jews. And then this distilled suffering will save the world.

MR. WIESEL:

That's a beautiful Talmudic image. Either Elijah or the Messiah.

CARDINAL O'CONNOR:

And yet you've said, I must admit very clearly, that you cannot consider suffering a gift. My statement was theological, but I must confess, I was deeply hurt.

ELIE WIESEL:

We, we met the next day.

CARDINAL O'CONNOR:

Oh, you were marvelous. You came to see me because you knew what I meant.

ELIE WIESEL:

Yes. And I simply suggested that instead of "gift," the word "lesson."

CARDINAL O'CONNOR:

Yes.

ELIE WIESEL:

I understood, in your terminology naturally, what it means.

CARDINAL O'CONNOR:

That was one of the most touching things that you did, to come to see me the next day, and—

MR. PRESSMAN:

You compared the Holocaust, or the suffering of the Jewish people, to the Crucifixion at one point, too.

CARDINAL O'CONNOR:

I have continued to do so, and I know that there are Jewish theologians who disagree with me. There are others who agree with me; there is a Jewish theologian, a rabbi, who wrote a very extensive article in the *Jewish Encyclopedia of Religion* on suffering. He understands precisely what I'm talking about, and doesn't see a dissonance in the comparison at all.

Of course for me the Crucifixion is the central act of my life; it has central meaning in my life; it dominates everything that I do. And it led to the Resurrection. You talked about the miracle or the mystery of the renaissance of Israel. And even though some would disagree with me, I'm haunted by the fact that no one has been able to explain the mystery of the Holocaust. No one has been able to explain the mystery of the sufferings of Christ.

People operating on the basis of human reason justifiably said, "If you're the Son of God, prove it by coming down from the cross. Prove it by renouncing suffering." And he didn't. It takes us back to the question of how could God tolerate evil? How could God let the Holocaust happen? I don't know. It's a mystery. I can't believe it's a meaningless mystery. I can't believe that there's no power in it. So I appreciate what you're saying in calling it a lesson. And yet I persist in believing there's something more than that.

MR. PRESSMAN:

You said recently, Mr. Wiesel: "I speak of society's attraction to violence on the one hand and the temptation of suicide on the other. How can we explain the hate that burns in so many homes?" And then you went on to say that all roads lead us back to Auschwitz. "Defying all analogies, Auschwitz institutes itself as a point of reference because it symbolizes the culmination of violence, hatred and death." You feel that the violence in our society today is somehow related to Auschwitz, don't you?

MR. WIESEL:

I believe everything is. If in those years it was possible for six million Jews to be killed in the twentieth century, that means something was wrong with the world. And therefore, it overlapped—the cup runneth over. The violence from there and then is still here. The hatred from there and then is still here.

And so, to me, it is a mystery. What happened then is the central mystery of life, and of history. On all levels, human and psychological and theological.

MR. PRESSMAN:

Some phrases from your life, Mr. Wiesel: "I believe during the Holocaust, the covenant was broken."

MR. WIESEL:

I placed that statement in a certain context. I said the following: that God and the Jews and Israel, the people of Israel, had a covenant. We were supposed to observe and to protect His law. And He was supposed to protect us. And

69

since He didn't protect us, we had the feeling that the covenant was broken. But the next step is the realization that we cannot live without that covenant. I think the Jewish people cannot live without that covenant.

And from the beginnings of our history, this has been the motivation to redeem the world and to redeem God through our celebration of life, of the law—through our celebration of humanity. But I see the picture here, and I cannot not comment on it, you know. Jerusalem is the dream of my dream. Strangely enough, before I ever came to Jerusalem, I had been in Jerusalem. And nevertheless, every time I go to Jerusalem, it's like the first time.

And every time I come to the Wall—I always go to the Western Wall—I'm overcome by such emotion that I feel that the emotion preceded me. As if I had been there for centuries and centuries and centuries.

CARDINAL O'CONNOR:

In the Passover seder, the father or the patriarch, the man presiding or the woman, nowadays, says, "We're doing this tonight"—paraphrasing—"because of what . . . God did for us in Egypt"—as though he was there.

MR. WIESEL:

Right. We are supposed to believe we were there. Every Jew is supposed to believe that he stood at Sinai, hearing God's word. What a wonderful thing it is for a Jew to have God's voice in his or her memory.

CARDINAL O'CONNOR:

But God doesn't break his promise. He didn't break that covenant. That's why it's a mystery. If it were an algebraic

70

equation, if you could write it as a mathematical equation, it wouldn't be a mystery. I can't understand it but God didn't break his promise.

When you talk about suffering spilling over, Leon Bloy, a French Jew who became a Catholic, wrote about the crucifixion in *The Woman Who Was Poor,* a powerful book which opens with that shocking scene: the drunk sitting on the step of the church saying, "This place stinks of God." He says that at the Crucifixion, the animals themselves, rabbits and hyenas and jackals and lions and turtles, the fish of the sea, they all went into a cataclysm of suffering, so catastrophic was the reversal of all order. This was because the one that we believe to be the Son of God was crucified.

How can we accept that concept? Should we say that God broke his covenant with his son? No. We don't understand it. It's a mystery. That's faith. Why did the Jewish people keep going when they thought God had abandoned them in the desert? When they were hungry, when they were starving? When they complained to Moses?

MR. WIESEL:

In the Jewish tradition, we frequently ask the question, "Has God abandoned us?" In Ezekiel especially and other prophets, we ask: Why did you forsake us? Some elders of Israel were afraid that God may have abandoned us. The fear is always there. What does it teach us? That questions are valid. Answers are not. And that we have the right to ask the question.

MR. PRESSMAN:

The problems of contemporary society, the problem of violence—how do those problems relate to the Holocaust?

MR. WIESEL:

I could spend more than a few hours to show you the relationship. The indifference today to other people's suffering is a reflection of the indifference shown to Jewish people's suffering. Take the skinheads. They are using Nazi vocabulary. Why do they use swastikas?

Somehow, all those who practice evil today, in every land, feel that they must link their evil deeds to Nazism. And I think the lesson is not to be indifferent, and to help, and if people suffer, to speak up and not allow that suffering to continue.

MR. PRESSMAN:

Are you concerned, both of you, as New Yorkers, about the growth of racism, of black-white conflict in our own community?

CARDINAL O'CONNOR:

I find, again, that it is deep-rooted. Institutionalized. Much of it operates at the unconscious level.

Of course, progress has been made, just as progress has been made in regard to anti-Semitism. But it certainly hasn't been rooted out. I'll tell you why it hasn't been rooted out. I'm often asked what's wrong with the city, what's wrong with the country. And my answer is always the same, and it sounds like a platitude. We have yet to come to recognize the sacredness, the worth, the dignity of every human person.

And racism hasn't been rooted out because we haven't had anything to replace it with. We haven't replaced it with the sense of the sacred. Anti-Semitism continues. We haven't rooted it out. We haven't replaced it with the sense of the sacredness of the human person. We still accept subway cars that are better fit for cattle than human persons; we accept crime in the streets, all sorts of violence because we still have a great deal of contempt for, or at least a lack of a sense of the sacredness of the human person.

MR. WIESEL:

I am as aware, as concerned and troubled—but it's not only in New York, it's all over. In France, Le Pen and his followers are racists. In Germany, the gypsies are still being persecuted. And the Turks are being discriminated against. In Britain, the prejudice is against Asians. In every country, the stranger is still arousing suspicion and hatred. And New York being the city par excellence, the metropolis of the world, of course everything here is emphasized and magnified.

I am terribly worried about the racial tensions in our midst. What to do about them? I believe in encounters. I believe in dialogue. We need to arrange more meetings between blacks and whites and Jews and Hispanics and Koreans—and make all aware that something is happening.

MR. PRESSMAN:

Do you think it's getting worse?

MR. WIESEL:

I cannot tell you. I don't know enough; I'm not a social scientist. But I'm worried enough to say that it's an emergency situation. That we may not allow it to continue, because if it does, if it continues, it's going to become worse.

MR. PRESSMAN:

Black-white relations.

MR. WIESEL:

Interracial relations.

CARDINAL O'CONNOR:

Right.

MR. PRESSMAN:

In your Nobel speech, you said that apartheid was as abhorrent as anti-Semitism. Do you feel that what's still happening in South Africa is a threat to the stability of the whole world?

MR. WIESEL:

Well, surely if apartheid were to be abolished, it would help the world. For the moment it's still there. I think it's offensive. I was in South Africa in '75, to lecture, and of course I created antagonism; I spoke up against apartheid. I felt ashamed for being white. And I remember I had the same feeling when I came to the United States as a journalist, many, many years ago, and I went to the South.

Racism then was still the law of the land. I remember I was ashamed. I was ashamed of not being black. I think more should be done and said to denounce apartheid.

CARDINAL O'CONNOR:

Archbishop Tutu has been to see me two or three times. The first time he came, we had a very private discussion and he showed me his passport that wasn't a passport. It was simply a document that permitted him to travel. He couldn't have a passport because in accordance with South African law he's not a national. He's a "colored." The effort there has been to divide, therefore to conquer, by categorizing whole groups.

They give you a piece of paper which says if you are a colored, you're a non-person. You're not a South African and therefore you can't have a passport. This is a frightening reality.

MR. WIESEL:

It is an abomination.

MR. PRESSMAN:

In a recent article, Mr. Wiesel, you asked: Are we afraid of peace? And you suggested that peace remains an elusive goal because statesmen skilled at waging war lack the dedication, the humanity, to find a way to avoid war.

MR. WIESEL:

[*Sighs*] Well, on one hand, we are lucky. There has been no major war since 1945. But we are unlucky, because there have been, I think, fifty or sixty "small" wars in the world. And every war—I totally agree with you—every war is a wrong war. Except for the Allies' war against Hitler. Which was a just war. Had I been in the United States or Britain,

I would have enlisted, no doubt, to fight Hitler and fascism and evil.

But otherwise, all wars today are the wrong wars. Everybody's losing. And everybody's a victim.

MR. PRESSMAN:

Do you fear that there can be a nuclear holocaust, despite the apparent rapprochement between the Soviet Union and the United States? The proliferation of nuclear weapons—can that lead to war?

MR. WIESEL:

Yes. Look: the *Challenger,* after all, exploded. Chernobyl exploded. The nuclear submarine, the Russian one, exploded—which means accidents can happen. Which means we are not safe in the air, in the sea, and on the ground. And I think history is teaching us a lesson there, to be careful with nuclear weapons. What I am afraid of, really, are the small nations. Just imagine someone like Idi Amin or Bokassa, the leader of some small country that would acquire nuclear weapons. They wouldn't wait. Take Iraq-Iran—if Iraq had nuclear weapons, don't you think it would have used them against Iran? And once used, a chain reaction would follow. And that would be the end of humanity. That is my fear.

MR. PRESSMAN:

Is it yours as well, Your Eminence?

CARDINAL O'CONNOR:

I couldn't spend all those years in uniform without being afraid of an accidental detonation, and I have seen too many weapons fired awry, too many systems break down; I've seen human beings break down. If you stockpile weapons in such multitudes, there's no way in God's world that you can categorically defend against error.

I, too, fear a terroristic use. Look what has happened in the Middle East with chemical warfare. This is a perfect illustration. My fear of nuclear warfare, as the probable rupture of peace or a deterrent to true peace, however, is not so great as that which was singled out by Mother Theresa of Calcutta. Most people don't want to talk about what she said, because it looks as though you're attacking individual women.

But in her address at the Nobel Prize ceremony, she said the greatest enemy to peace in the world is abortion. And I honestly believe this. I believe that we have created a mentality of violence, a mentality in which we have lost respect for the sacredness of the human person. I do not mean that an individual woman is to be condemned because of confusion or anxiety, or because of her beliefs. Maybe she doesn't believe that the baby within is truly human. So that's not what I'm talking about. I'm talking about massive manipulated propagandized movements that have brought about more than a million and a half unborn deaths every year.

It is very difficult to maintain the peace and tranquility in light of this, and I know that the problem continues.

MR. PRESSMAN:

Do you see abortion as a manifestation of violence in our society, Mr. Wiesel?

MR. WIESEL:

I must confess I do not share the Cardinal's strong feelings. I understand why you feel that way. I do not. I am not saying I am for or against. I have to think about it much more, and I really have not given the issue enough thought. But even if I were against abortion, I would not compare it to a nuclear conflagration.

CARDINAL O'CONNOR:

No, I didn't do that. We were talking about threats to peace, and I thought we had gotten off the question of the nuclear threat. But you know, I read what to me was a very chilling alleged finding in the papers the other day, even though I'm very skeptical of polls. This one alleged that some 56 percent of women polled believe that abortion is murder but that it should be a woman's right. Now, intellectually I can't accept that kind of reasoning. I realize that there are those whose faith tells them that up to a certain point, this growth is not a human being. They're not the ones I'm talking about here. I honestly believe that they have an obligation to reevaluate their position in the light of so much scientific evidence that the unborn *is* a human being. I'm talking at this point, however, about those who say they believe abortion is murder, but think that it should be a woman's right. To me that doesn't make sense.

MR. WIESEL:

The debate on abortion has not been a debate on a high level. I have read articles for and against, violent articles for and against, but the debate that needs to be held must deal with the moral aspects. I don't like the violence of the debate that's been held so far.

CARDINAL O'CONNOR:

I don't like the violence of the debate, and I don't like the violence of abortion. But I don't like the fact either that there are women who don't know where to turn. We have all sorts of programs in the Archdiocese of New York to try to help women who are confused and perplexed.

MR. PRESSMAN:

Right now the people of New York State and those in other parts of the country are confronted with the question of capital punishment. Should it be resumed? In your book *Dawn,* you wrote how the grizzled master had explained the Sixth Commandment. Why has a man no right to commit murder? Because in so doing he takes upon himself the function of God, and this must not be done too easily. Are you against capital punishment?

MR. WIESEL:

I am against capital punishment, yes. I am against death. I feel it's wrong, the whole institution is wrong. I know violent crimes call for an answer, but capital punishment is the wrong answer. I am against it.

There may be some exceptions. For instance, when Israel decided to execute Eichmann, I was for it. I imagine if somebody was to kill, I don't know, twenty or thirty children, I would have to think about it again. But in principle, I am against institutionalized death.

MR. PRESSMAN:

What about you, Your Eminence?

CARDINAL O'CONNOR:

The position of the bishops of the United States is very clear; the Church's position is clear. The bishops of New York have been very clear that the Church accepts the authority of the state to carry out the death penalty, but the bishops of the United States have repeatedly urged against the use of the death penalty.

Professor Wiesel, you used two fascinating examples, one about Eichmann, the other about a killer of children. I listened to both of them. Certainly you're opposed to war as such. War as such is an evil. Is it the greater or the lesser of evils at any given time? I cannot imagine anyone in his right mind, or her right mind, saying that we should not have gone to war against the Nazis.

Now, at times, the means that were used, carpet bombing, obliteration bombing, this was a very questionable thing, because there were innocent civilians who were killed. You used an illustration about capital punishment. You are against death. And of course you are against capital punishment because you are against death. But there are exceptions, and you used Eichmann as an exception.

This is what the Church says, that the Church is certainly opposed to putting innocent people to death, even if for no other reason than that we think a civilized nation has to find better ways of handling crime than to put people to death. Of course, there *are* other reasons.

MR. PRESSMAN:

In this case, you're not for the legislature overriding the governor's veto?

CARDINAL O'CONNOR:

The bishops of New York have gone on record. They have publicized the position that the state has the right to put people to death, but the bishops urge against the exercise of that right. I won't say I'm against overriding the veto or not overriding the veto, because it's very difficult when you get into such a situation to present purely a moral argument. If they will let us present purely a moral argument, and assure us that there are no political implications involved, then I'll be very happy to give a definitive statement about something of that sort.

MR. PRESSMAN:

Religion and politics. Do you think that they should be separate?

CARDINAL O'CONNOR:

I think what we generally mean when we say "religion" is distorted and falsified, perverted. What we mean by "politics" is something quite different. If you're referring to the body politic, if you're referring to the articulation of public policy, then if you divorce the moral or the religious from the explication of public policy, I'd say of course, you can't do that.

If you're talking about "political" in the almost pejorative sense in which we so often speak, unfortunately, about politicians, then churchmen should not be politicians. It's not the responsibility of churchmen to legislate; it's not the responsibility of churchmen to sit in civil courts and offer judicial decisions or opinions. It's not the role of the Church to formulate public policy for all of the people.

Look at the criticism that the Church has been subject to, back in the days of Nazi Germany. There were churchmen who did protest. There were churchmen who didn't protest. This has always haunted me, and whenever I've had to ask myself a question, should you leap into this arena of public policy that's being formed, or public policy that is in existence—I ask the reverse question: what right do I have as a highly visible churchman to be silent about a public policy that I think may be bad for the people? That may be immoral? That may adversely affect the people? That's one of my reasons for arguing so strongly in public against abortion. If I believe, as I do, that it is the taking of innocent human life, how could I live with myself if I kept silent?

MR. PRESSMAN:

You talked earlier, Mr. Wiesel, about the Nobel ceremony and the link between your father and your son, Shlomo, who came up to the podium with you.

MR. WIESEL:

Shlomo Elisha.

MR. PRESSMAN:

Shlomo Elisha. Do you think you've been true to both your father and your son in your life?

MR. WIESEL:

I am trying. All my life I am trying. I don't think I succeeded very well. But I'm trying. I am trying to keep some memories alive, I am trying to communicate a certain distaste for violence. I am trying to bring people together. But then, as survivors, as teachers—that is what we are doing, that is what we are supposed to do.

Have I justified the hope my father had in me? I'm not sure. If there had been no war, I may well have become head of a small yeshiva, teaching Talmud and writing biblical commentaries. Maybe he would have preferred me that way.

As for my son, I can tell you one thing. Since he was born, I have become doubly involved in public affairs. Because I brought a life into this world, it's my duty to try to make the world better for him.

MR. PRESSMAN:

Has it been difficult for your son to be your son?

MR. WIESEL:

He wouldn't want me to speak about him.

MR. PRESSMAN:

You seldom do.

MR. WIESEL:

I seldom do. But I am crazy about my son. I could use all kinds of examples, but he's my life and in a way I owe my life to him, as much as I owe it to my father. So I know I am placing a tremendous burden on his shoulders, and it's unfair. He's a young boy, sixteen, and I am putting upon his shoulders—myself and my father and two thousand years of Jewish history. He wants to go and play baseball!

MR. PRESSMAN:

Immortality? Do you see in him?

MR. WIESEL:

Oh, no . . . I do see in him my father, but I am not going so far as to say immortality; I see my father there, and the most important element is really that he makes me vulnerable and strong at the same time. Because of him I would do many things. At the same time if, God forbid, something would happen to him, I would be crushed. He would not like to hear it, but it's true. I come back from the other side of the world to spend a Shabbat with him, because I feel that if he is here, I have no right not to spend the Sabbath with him, not to give myself to him and not to try to improve the world around him.

MR. PRESSMAN:

Nat Hentoff has said to you, "There's no question in my mind but that John Cardinal O'Connor would be much happier as a pastor, starting the rosary at wakes, making a retarded child smile, visiting the sick and giving Sunday homilies that other priests might consider too long, but there'd be few complaints from the laity." True or false?

CARDINAL O'CONNOR:

I think I would be very happy as a parish priest. That's all I ever wanted to be. It sounds again like a cliché, it sounds like false modesty, false humility. So many Catholics, so many priests, nuns, others, think—"Gee, the Cardinal, Archbishop of New York, he's in one of the most visible and prestigious positions in the world." They use a term that I abhor, one of the most "powerful" positions in the world. But I try to do the work of a parish priest right now. I try to make retarded children smile, literally. I go to wakes. I lead the rosary. I try to do these things that I would do if I were a parish priest. Obviously, I have to be distanced from so very much of that.

MR. PRESSMAN:

When you were a child, you found a great interest in retarded children, didn't you?

CARDINAL O'CONNOR:

Yes. That was my first love, and I have great admiration for families who take loving care of a retarded child. And I see how such a child will bring families together.

I'm thinking about what Professor Wiesel said before— that you virtually died, life stopped for you when your father died. And now you say, in essence, life would stop for you if your son died. Recently I was talking with a number of our priests, and I made the point to them that in the Arab world, as you would well know, the son prefixes his name with *Ibn*, 'son of' and then the father with *Ab*, 'father of.' That's how intimate the relationship is. I'm very touched by what you said. It's a wonderful thing to see a loving relationship and a relationship that is so close that life would virtually stop if one were deprived of it.

That's what the parish priest, I think, comes to feel about his people. They are virtually his life's blood. He has no natural children; they are his supernatural sons and daughters and that's the way I have to try to feel. Otherwise, I would have practically no life. I don't have that kind

85

of perfection, to be able to relate only to God. I have to relate to God's people.

I wish I could say, even with your certitude, that you try to do what your father would have wanted. Sometimes I think I don't even try adequately to do and to be what I should do and should be.

MR. WIESEL:

You know which word is the most frequent in the Bible? It's not *God,* but *ben* ('son of ———').

CARDINAL O'CONNOR:

Ben, sure. Sure.

MR. PRESSMAN:

One more photo—a symbolic picture from your installation?

CARDINAL O'CONNOR:

Young John O'Connor. That was another one of those completely spontaneous things.

MR. PRESSMAN:

The boy was your namesake.

CARDINAL O'CONNOR:

He was my namesake. As soon as it was announced that I'd been appointed Archbishop of New York, this lad wrote to me. He told me that the next day was his birthday, and he told me about his grandfather, his mother and father. I got the phone number and his address in New York, and I called him.

And it was funny because first his father answered. I said, "This is Bishop O'Connor in Scranton." And his father didn't believe me. So then his mother got on the line. His mother had almost equal difficulty in believing me. But finally I got the little boy on the line. So when I was going to be installed in the cathedral on the nineteenth of March of 1984, I invited this little boy and his family to the ceremony. When I got up into the pulpit, one of those crazy thoughts hit me, and I never had that kind of discipline to stop myself.

So I called the boy up; he had to climb up these steps and nobody knew what was going on. And I took my miter, as it's called, and put it on him. It was a moment of indescribable joy!